Cared For:

The amazing story of Three Little Birds

KATIE DAUER

Balboa Press books may be ordered through booksellers or by contacting:

Balboa Press
A Division of Hay House
1663 Liberty Drive
Bloomington, IN 47403
www.balboapress.com
844-682-1282

Interior Image Credit: Katie Dauer

ISBN: 979-8-7652-4898-0 (sc)
ISBN: 979-8-7652-4899-7 (e)

Library of Congress Control Number: 2024900748

Print information available on the last page.

Balboa Press rev. date: 01/15/2024

BALBOA.PRESS
A DIVISION OF HAY HOUSE

Once upon a time, our mama birdie found a very
safe truck trailer where she could build a nest.

It hadn't been driven for several years, so our mama built a nest beneath it and laid three eggs.

We baby birds had just hatched, and our mama was taking good care of us. She had gone out to look for food when suddenly we felt movement and heard the loud sound of the truck starting its motor.

My two siblings, Rusty and Tiny, were very scared as the large vehicle took off down the road. I chirped at them, and we snuggled down in the nest to protect ourselves from falling during the long ride. We wondered how our mama felt when she came back with our food and we were no longer there.

We felt so many emotions—sadness at worrying about our mama; fear about this long, noisy, bumpy ride; and anxiety about not knowing when we would eat again.

After two hours, the movement stopped, and the noise was gone. It seemed as if we were in a building. We heard people talking. We chirped a lot because we were so hungry. Suddenly there were two humans shining a flashlight at us. We were frightened but happy to think they would give us some food.

4

The human man found a box, and he carefully put our whole nest in the box. The gentle lady held the box and took us to her house.

We could hear her talking and knew she was trying to figure out how to help us. She learned that we could eat dog kibbles but that she should not feed us worms or give us water. This sweet lady didn't have dogs, but she had a couple of cats. So she took some cat food and moistened it till it was very soft.

She then used her finger to feed these kibbles to Tiny, Rusty, and me (Robby) by putting them directly in our mouth.

The first few days and nights, we were very hungry, and our dependable lady fed us every two hours. After eating, we slept very soundly in our nest. We also pooped a lot. But our hardworking lady kept our box nice and clean.

We started growing out of our box, and one day the understanding lady put us in a cage with our nest. There, we had more room to flap our wings. She still fed us regularly and cleaned the cage often.

By now she was starting to give us water with her finger. She dipped her finger in water, and then we would grab it and get one drop at a time. She also placed a container with water in the cage. Initially we didn't know what to do with it. Occasionally the determined lady would dunk our beaks in water. Soon, we learned how to drink on our own.

Our motherly lady touched us with so much gentleness and love. We thought it felt just like it would have if our birdie mama would have been able to love and touch us.

Tiny, Rusty, and I stayed very warm and well fed. However, Tiny wasn't eating well and soon was not very strong. I remember the day the passionate lady took him out of the cage and just snuggled with him. He felt loved and took his last breath in her hands. She buried him in a box in their yard. We felt sad for Tiny but knew that he had been loved.

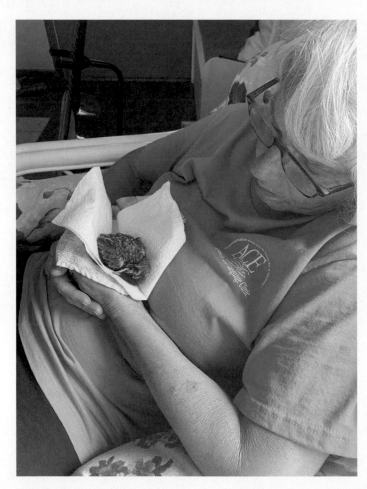

One day, our adventurous lady put us in the car, and we drove awhile; she even fed us in the car.

We went to a cabin, and the kind lady set us free in a room. We loved looking out the windows; it was a new adventure for us.

There she also let us outside, but we weren't strong enough to fly away. We stayed close.

Then in a couple of days, we rode back home. Our protective lady let us out into a little house for their kitties, called a cattio, and we were able to try to fly there. We did do a little flying but were still not strong enough to take off.

When our thoughtful lady would feed us, she would take us out of the cage and place us in a large container with the food and water so we had more room. After she gave us the food and water with her finger, sometimes we would venture out and try to start flying in the room. We were getting stronger. We were also getting bigger and had all our feathers.

We know that over the course of her caring for us, our kind lady fell in love with us, and she had a very hard time thinking of letting us go.

But one night, three humans—including our wise lady—took us out to a park. She took us out of the cage and fed us in the box.

When we had eaten our fill, Rusty and I flew up on our supportive lady's shoulder. We stood there awhile and pooped on her, and then we both flew off.

We had lived because our strong, selfless lady took such good care of us, and then she also let us go.

20

We see her now and then down at the park, and we chirp at her and let her know that we thank her for her love and caring and for being brave enough to set us free.

The lady who found us and took care of us was gentle, sweet, dependable, hardworking, understanding, determined, motherly, passionate, adventurous, protective, thoughtful, kind, supportive, strong, and selfless, just like all moms.

We love you, kind lady. Thank you for adopting us.

Printed in the United States
by Baker & Taylor Publisher Services